To Eleanor,

*Faith, Courage,
and Survival
in a Time of Trouble*

With my
best wishes

8/12/2017

Faith, Courage, and Survival in a Time of Trouble

**By France J. Pruitt
as told to Judy Priven**

S2 PRESS, BETHESDA, MARYLAND

Published by:
S2 Press
P. O. Box 34430
Bethesda, Maryland 20827

Printed and distributed by:
Lulu.com
To order more copies, please go to:
http://www.lulu.com/content/155537

Library of Congress Control Number: 2005933925

ISBN Number: 978-1-4116-8230-6

Printed and bound in the United States of America

To the memory of my wonderful mother and father, André and Denise J., and to the people of the Cévennes who selflessly saved our lives.

TABLE OF CONTENTS

Acknowledgments

Our many thanks to Judy Priven for her patience and persistence in trying to understand the life story of her friend and preparing such a well crafted document, to Dean G. Pruitt for the many hours he spent carefully editing the manuscript, and Paul D. Pruitt for his excellent work as the publisher.

Note

To preserve the anonymity of certain members of the family, the last name of my parents has been rendered as J.

Introduction

The first part of this book tells the story of a Belgian family who spent more than four years during the Second World War as refugees in the south of France. The author was five years old when the family left Brussels and ten when they returned. At first, the family lived openly in a rented farm, supporting themselves as farmers. But they eventually had to go into hiding and were sheltered by families in the region who risked their lives by doing so.

The second part of the book describes the author's life after arriving in the United States.

The third part of the book takes the readers to June of 2005, when several members of the author's family returned to the region to dedicate a granite bench in honor of the courageous efforts of its people. Speeches, comments, and pictures from the dedication ceremony can be found at the end of the book, along with maps of the region and some family genealogies.

Foreword

*1933, a year to remember: Hitler was named Chancellor.
Germany was gradually building its military strength,
recovering from the occupation of the First World War.
Dachau, the first concentration camp, was built and the
boycott against Jews began around that time. Two years later,
the Jews in Germany lost their citizenship and civil rights,
Jewish kids were expelled from schools, and some Jews were
sent to concentration camps. Things got worse for the next six
years, culminating in the invasion of Poland in 1939 and the
invasion of France and the Low Countries the following spring.*

The author on holiday in Switzerland in 1939

Early Memories

I guess I will begin my story, and the story of my family, during World War II, in the same way that our seven-year-old granddaughter, Katie, started her book three years ago about the dream of a princess. Once upon a time...

Once upon a time, a princess was born. That was myself, France Ida Elizabeth, and I was born in September, 1934. I was not really a princess, of course, but my life seemed charmed right from the beginning, as though I really were a princess.

The year before, my father and mother were married in Antwerp, Belgium, first in a civil ceremony at City Hall and then in a Jewish ceremony at the Salle Centenaire, to please their grandparents on both sides. Their wedding, too, seemed to come right from a book of fairy tales. It was a double wedding—a ceremony in which two brothers, André and Alex, married two sisters, Denise and Andrée. André, my father, was a highly respected chemistry professor, well-liked by his students at the Free University of Brussels (l'Université Libre de Bruxelles.) Alex, my uncle, was a successful stamp dealer who was continuing the work started by his father.

Although the two sisters, Denise and Andrée, were highly intelligent, neither of them attended a university—as was customary for girls in those days.

All of Antwerp's best-known citizens, including the mayor himself, attended the star-touched wedding as my grandfather was a very successful diamond businessman in the city. But this was Europe in 1933 and Fate had a few surprises for us all. Who would have guessed that the Antwerp Jewish community, as we knew it, would disappear in a just a few years? Who would have guessed that, I, that lucky baby princess, would experience hunger, cold, complete helplessness, and great fear for my life, or that I would be violated—not once but two times—before I was ten years old? And all because of a religion that no one in my parents' generation and their parents ever practiced or even believed in.

It is only now, 71 years after I was born, that I realize how easy my life really has been all along. Has it been charmed because of that same Fate that robbed me of my childhood and dealt me such hardship at such an early age? Or because of my parents' faith and courage in leaving their comfortable life in Brussels? Or the selflessness and kindness of the people of the Cévennes for taking such good care of us for four years? Or the choices I made in life? No one can say.

My Parents

Neither of my parents was religious, although Belgium at the time was 90 percent Catholic, with a government that was pretty much dominated by the Church. As a liberal thinker and a Free Mason, my father believed strongly in the separation of Church and State. He felt so strongly about it that he created a club at the University called the Circle of Free Examination, whose sole goal was to allow people to exchange ideas and to test their ways of comprehending the world. If I understand it correctly, that club still exists.

My father was the first one in his family to earn a Doctoral degree. Because he was a brilliant student and later an astute researcher at the Belgian Research Institute, he was offered a position as chemistry professor at the Free University of Brussels. Like most Belgians, he worked very hard, even on Saturdays (until noon); Sunday, at least, was a day of rest.

In his late 20's, he met a medium who was able to convince him that there was something in the world beyond scientific findings. Later, he observed how the "guerisseurs" (healers) in the south of France were able to heal. These experiences made him very interested in matters that could not be explained scientifically.

He was a gentle and caring man who was interested in many topics and loved good discussions. In the latter part of his life, he always had a retinue of people, especially ladies, who wanted to spend time with him because he was so genuinely interested in them and such a good conversationalist. He was quite advanced spiritually, which showed in his attitude toward life.

My mother may not have been religious in the traditional sense of the word, but she had a deep and sincere love for everyone she met. And everyone she met also loved her—her compassion, her understanding, her care, her complete selflessness. When her own mother died, she was the one who stayed at home and took care of her 16-year-old sister Andrée and her 8-year old brother Francis. My mother was only 18 at the time.

Although she had been a brilliant student in high school and had dreams of going to medical school, like almost all young ladies of her status, she did not attend an institution of higher education and never worked outside the home. My Aunt Andrée, on the other hand, was the more rebellious of the two sisters and went to a Paris finishing school for a year after her graduation from high school—a very unusual decision. I think she felt overwhelmed by my mother's self-confidence and popularity. It was not until years later, after my mother died, that my aunt cast off the shadow of her sister and began to blossom as the warm and giving person she must have felt inside all along.

My father and mother got along famously; in fact, I never heard a word of discord between them. They loved to read to each other and take long walks.

They lived a comfortable life, owning an apartment in one of the nicer parts of Brussels, right across from a well manicured park. We often went to the park and made friends with many people, including a guard. We had a lot of family members in Brussels whom we often visited. We were always nicely dressed and wore white gloves when we went to the Sunday afternoon teas with our grandparents.

In the winter time, we went to Switzerland to ski and in the summer we went to the Belgian seashore even if it was not always that warm.

Like many other Belgians, we celebrated Christmas at home with a family feast but, of course, we did not go to church. (In Belgium the distribution of presents, especially to children, is done on St Nicolas Day, the 6th of December, rather than on Christmas Day.)

My uncle and father hard at work
at La Font, our farm in the south of France

On Our Way

In the late '30's, most Jews in Belgium and the rest of Europe were oblivious to and unperturbed by the events in Germany, but the two brothers and their wives, listening to the BBC and reading the newspapers, saw the handwriting on the wall—for Germany and for the rest of western Europe. I am not sure why they saw the future more clearly than those around them. Perhaps my father's interest in psychology played some part. He and his brother were also wise enough not to be attached to material things, which led to the demise of so many other people, including quite a few of our relatives.

In any case, the two brothers began planning their escape. But where to go? Their first thought was England, since my mother and aunt were British subjects.

My maternal grandfather, one of eleven children, was born in Scotland and went to England as a young man. His father was born in Russia and had emigrated to Scotland. My grandfather lived in Belgium most of his adult life except during the two world wars, when he lived in England and became a successful diamond dealer. In 1940, at the age of 20, my uncle Francis, my mother's brother, who was a university student in Belgium, left for Britain on the last ship that departed France. He immediately joined the British Royal Air Force.

England was willing to accept the two sisters and their father but, sad to say, not their husbands. Since my father and uncle were respectively, Belgian and Dutch citizens, they did not have the birthright credentials with which to claim asylum in any country outside those that were likely to be occupied by the Nazis.

Their next thought was France, to which they could easily escape. Somewhere in France, they thought, would be a place that could provide some measure of safety. To get there, they decided to flee in my maternal grandfather's black Buick, which was large enough to fit the whole family. (In fact, my grandfather was driven around in this car by a chauffeur, since he didn't know how to drive.)

And so, the two couples, who by 1940 had two children each, put their furniture in storage, sold their apartments in Brussels, and moved to the Belgian coast, close to the border, with my paternal grandfather and grandmother. There they waited to leave the country for the time when my father would be free to leave the University.

And then it happened. On May 10, 1940, Germany invaded the Netherlands, Belgium and Luxemburg. My father, who was released from his University services that day, ran to the bank to pick up the diamonds my maternal grandfather had given to the family. But there was one problem: arriving at the bank, he realized he did not know the password for the safe because his brother Alex was in charge of the diamonds. So he guessed. By a stroke of luck, and that story was mentioned to us afterwards on numerous occasions, he guessed correctly. The password was his brother's own name—Alex. This was fortunate, because those diamonds turned out to be the only portable wealth available to the family for the next four years. Neither my father nor my uncle was able to continue his career and earn money for the four and a half years of the war.

On the day of the invasion, all trains in Belgium had stopped running, so, with the diamonds in his briefcase, my father bicycled three hours to the coast. The next day, the whole family piled into the car—my father and uncle and paternal grandfather in the front (there were bench seats those days); my aunt and mother and paternal grandmother in the back; and we four children, all under six years old, on jump seats or sometimes on laps. Seat belts and air bags did not exist in those days, which made it a little easier for children to move around. And there were no radios or DVD players to entertain us. In this way, we set off for France along with thousands of other Belgians who were trying to escape the German army.

Behind the Buick was a trailer filled with all the worldly goods we had been able to assemble—clothes, blankets, and food. We didn't know exactly where we were going, and we didn't know what would happen to us. All we could rely on were our luck, our wits, the kindness of some strangers along the way—and my maternal grandfather's diamonds.

For me, the beginning of fear of the war started on that first night. We were traveling through an area that was clogged with refugees but empty of any stores, restaurants, or hotels. As afraid as I was, no one could comfort or reassure me, because everyone experienced that same fear of what would happen on that night and the days and nights to follow.

Because the border between the two countries was closed, we had to stop along the banks of a Belgian canal for

the night. I still remember the fear of the unknown darkness.
All was quiet except for the loud humming of the airplanes just
above us. My mother laid me down on the grass to sleep, but
suddenly, in the middle of the night, I woke up to find myself
rolling toward the canal. I can still remember the water coming
at me, dangerously close, before my mother grabbed me.

On the next day, we arrived at the border between
Belgium and France. My father, who was in the Belgian army
reserve, planned to go back to Brussels in case he was called
for duty; but, fortunately, the border police told him that the
Belgian capitulation was imminent and advised him to continue
on to France. Later, we found out that the border between
Belgium and France had been open for only 24 hours. We were
just very lucky.

After we entered France we stayed for one night at a
place called Andelices and then stopped for a week just south
of Paris in a chateau owned by a friend of my aunt. Perhaps we
could have stayed there longer, but my parents could not shake
the fear that Paris too would fall. And they were right.

Soon after we continued on south, a mandate went out
requiring all young men to build trenches around Paris. If my
father and uncle had been recruited for that effort, we all might
have perished, as the two women did not know how to drive.
Fortunately, the French police did not come to the hotel where
we were staying that night, and the two fathers were not
recruited. Only one month later, the Germans walked into
Paris, unopposed, and France signed an armistice.

Mountainous countryside in the Cévennes

Southern France

Bèdoues

My parents, and my uncle and aunt decided to keep going south, toward the mountains. But where? We were looking for a place that was remote and not too crowded, a place that was least likely to attract attention and most likely to have strangers who would sympathize with refugees.

The department of Lozère (one of 90 departments, or counties, in France) seemed just right. Lozère's nickname is "le pays de misères" or the "country of misery," referring to the miseries of the Protestant Huguenots who fled there in the 17th century to escape religious persecution. Perhaps, my parents reasoned, the descendants of the Huguenots, who had found refuge there, would offer refuge to others.

And again, they were right. Lozère is a relatively sparsely populated, resource-poor, mountainous area in the Massif Central in the southern part of France. That region, which is called the Cévennes, is covered with chestnut trees. My parents assumed that the Germans would not dare to go there. They were right; instead, the Germans delegated their power to the local French authorities, who performed the basic duties required of them—but also helped those in need, including us.

As we drove through the western part of Lozère, we found a small village named Bèdoues located near Florac. My father approached the Mayor of Florac who had authority to place refugees. Was there any place in the village where we could live for a while—all ten of us? The Mayor found us a place to live, a large house that looked like a chateau and belonged to the Governor of Djibouti. In return, my father, being a chemist, promised to help the farmers in the village with agricultural problems such as growing beets and extracting sugar from them. Later, he even received a certificate of appreciation for having helped the community to turn their plums into prunes, thanks to his knowledge of chemistry.

In order to survive, we started a garden not only for ourselves but also to make money. My father had never touched a hoe; but we grew cabbage, carrots, lettuce, and beets and plucked apples, peaches, cherries, and plums from the orchards. He used fertilizer and was able to grow carrots, the length of which was the envy of the people of Bèdoues. Everyone worked in the garden—even I, who was still only five years old.

In a short time, my mother too became a celebrity. Stories about her generosity and quick common sense spread throughout the area. Once when she was on her way to sell some of our cherries in a neighboring town, a bus she was riding in broke down on a bridge going over a main stream, during a major storm. Aware of the danger of rushing waters, she urged everyone to leave the bus as quickly as possible. Two minutes later, it was washed away. Thanks to her, everyone was safe.

But once again my parents were not satisfied. Situated in a valley, Bèdoues was too open, not remote enough. And so we moved again.

Soleyrols

Traveling east, our family found and rented an abandoned farm, called La Font, perched on a mountain, 20 minutes by foot from a small isolated village called Soleyrols. The village had ten to twelve farms, a school, a café, and a butcher shop—and little else. I suppose my parents were relieved, or just tired of searching. When we were in Vialas June 2005, we were told that the arrival of our black Buick was a major event in the region, as no one had ever seen such a big car before. That car had to be hidden; so after taking out the battery, putting the acid in a jar, and removing the license plate and tires, the car was put on bricks in an abandoned barn, where it remained until the end of the war. Four years later, the battery, the acid, the license and the tires were returned to their original positions. With some gas, the car started immediately.

Soleyrols was located on a secondary road that linked two towns: Florac, next to Bèdoues where we had spent the summer, and Vialas, where there was a Huguenot temple. Vialas was about 3.5 miles from Soleyrols, an hour walk in good weather. One winter day, all of us almost perished on that road when we were caught in a fierce snowstorm.

After settling down in the farm, my family and I began to venture further away, trekking beyond our safe little home to Vialas, where we attended the Huguenot Temple and its Sunday school. We took active part in special festivities like Christmas pageants. Visiting Alès, which was a larger town in the next department to the east, was risky because the Germans were visible in the town. Even so, we sometimes took the two-hour bus ride there to run errands, such as trading diamonds for cash or visiting the dentist. We definitely were afraid to show our faces beyond that town.

For awhile our life seemed uneventful—at least to us children. School? The school my cousin Chantal and I attended was certainly not the kind my parents would have chosen back home in Belgium. Located in Soleyrols, it was a one-room schoolhouse, with a single teacher, Mr. André, and over 20 children in 12 different grades. As a city girl suddenly thrust into a farm community, I must have felt out of place at first, even though I had not gone to a day care or a school before. You might say that this was my first experience in adjusting to "cultural differences." But my memory of that school is a pleasant one. I remember well the monthly visits of a very nice man who came regularly to teach us French songs with his guitar.

The other memory, which is not so good, is an outing organized by the teacher to show us the flora and fauna of the local stream. This is where the older boys decided to imitate what animals do in the fields. (Fifty years later, we met one of those boys, now an older man, who remembered with great emotion our family's stay in the area.) Our mothers decided to take us out of the school after that incident. But we would not have stayed there much longer as by early 1943, the situation for Jews was deteriorating.

La Font

La Font, our home for two years, was isolated from the main roads and was very primitive. It had four rooms: a storage room at one end, a common room at the other end, and two bedrooms in between. The common room served as the kitchen, dining room, living room and playroom. There was an outside verandah onto which most of the rooms opened. The heating system consisted of a fireplace in the common room and animals—pigs, rabbits, goats, and chickens—underneath us. This meant that wood had to be cut on the farm to be always available for cooking and heating water. In the back of the kitchen, there was a faucet with running water, but we had no indoor toilet. Taking a bath meant standing in a bucket and sponging ourselves with water that had been heated on the hearth. Going to the toilet consisted of going outside in the woods. There were chamber pots available for late night needs.

From 1940 until early 1943, we lived openly in this isolated farm. Although my grandparents were renting a room in Soleyrols, they spent the days with us. Unfortunately, my grandfather died of a heart attack while cutting wood for the stove, soon after we arrived. He is buried in the local cemetery, where his gravestone says "Here lies Louis J., 1869-1941, in this hospitable land."

Food was a problem, since we did not always have enough to eat. In addition to our rations of sugar, flour, oil, coffee (and cigarettes), which we received legally for the first two and a half years, we had to rely on the food we could produce or store on the farm or could barter with our chestnuts and other farm products such as honey. Yet this was an iffy situation as my parents were still not very experienced in growing vegetables or raising animals for eggs and meat. I can still remember coming back from school hungry and seeing pots on the stove. Alas, when I looked inside, they were filled with laundry.

Fortunately, my father was soon able to establish again a mutually beneficial relationship with the local villagers. He showed them how to make soap from grease and to extract sugar from beets. And in return, they showed us how to run the farm—namely, how to raise goats, rabbits, and chickens, collect the abundant chestnuts, dry them for the winter, plant the garden, and collect hay for the animals.

Collecting honey from the beehives was a specialized and delicate task in which my mother became the expert. Each year, we also had two pigs, whose main food was our garbage, supplemented by chestnuts. One year, we named them Hermann and Goering, for the hated Nazi official, as we knew we would have to kill them for our sustenance. When the time came to do so, the whole village came to help—gladly. Together, they all cleaned the intestines to make blood sausage, prepared gelatin with the hoofs and pate with the liver. We had electricity but no refrigerators or freezers, so the meat was stored with the local butcher or bartered.

There were many foods that we children collected in the fields, such as dandelions for salads and mushrooms to add to stews. We learned to distinguish the poisonous one from those that could be eaten.

Chestnuts were the main crop of the farm and appeared on the table at every meal. Picking them up in the fall was a full-time occupation for the whole family. I can still remember how the prickly outer layer of the chestnuts often hurt our fingers badly. To preserve the chestnuts for year-around food, we had to dry them in a special two-story house where a low fire was kept for a whole month. Once dried, they had to be boiled for over two hours before they could be eaten. Then they were served with milk and were really delicious. I still like the Bajanat, the patois name for that dish.

One treat was the sardines and dry fruit that my maternal Uncle Paul, who was living in the US, sent us every month for the first two years. He had immigrated earlier to the US and was able to send us those packages through Portugal. For us, candies did not exist, so that dried fruit was the only dessert we ever had. My parents tried to make it a real treat by telling us that we were getting 36,000 desserts. I never tired of those dried fruit and I still like them today. When I see how much food I have to bring into the house for our current sustenance, I often wonder how my parents brought everything they could not grow, on their backs from Soleyrols, to feed 10 people every day. Paper products did not exist, so we had to use leaves to clean ourselves and blow our noses.

The Maurel Family

Among the many friends we made was the Maurel family. Madame Maurel was a teacher in Alès who had a summer home in Vialas. She had two children: 18-year-old Max, with whom I fell in love (I was only seven at that time), and 16-year-old Fanchon, who became my best friend. One of my earliest memories of Max is when he took me around Alès on his motorcycle. Later he became a member of the Résistance and helped organize and negotiate our stay in various homes after we no longer could stay at the farm.

The relationship between the two families started in Vialas on a Sunday afternoon. Fanchon, who often tells the story, noted that my Sunday dress was spoiled and offered to clean it for my father. He had not been too successful in removing a berry stain on my white dress. The Maurels often visited us at La Font, bringing food, and providing the intellectual stimulation that my parents were missing. Fanchon taught us how to make dresses with chestnut leaves, and we all thought that was quite a treat, as we had so few toys.

My father and uncle also became very interested in the new field of psychology, influenced by their visit to a medium in Belgium. They and their wives started to design a system to classify people's personalities and values. This was a major topic of discussion during those visits with the Maurels.

Fanchon and I still call each other sisters and we have kept in touch for the past 60 years. We often entertain members of her family when they visit the US, and they entertain us when we visit Paris or Vialas. We were all very sad when we heard that Max passed away last fall just after his 80th birthday.

During the long evenings, when they were not too exhausted from physical labor, my father and uncle also read books about homeopathic medicine and stocked up on medications for potential sicknesses, as there were no doctors around. Later when we were in hiding, the medicines saved my sister's life when she fell down a flight of stairs and had a serious concussion, along with symptoms of meningitis. Later, I fell on a nail in a barn where there was plenty of manure; once again, my father and uncle's stores of medicine came in handy, since I was surely not caught up with my tetanus shots. Fortunately too, we were not exposed to many other kids so we did not catch any of the childhood diseases. I do not actually recall visiting a doctor during those four years, an amazing phenomenon when I see how often my grandchildren have to visit the doctor nowadays.

My Brother's Birth

In the spring of 1942, my brother was born. My parents chose the name Cristian mainly because they liked it, rather than for religious reasons.

My mother, sister, and I had to go to Aubenas, a larger town located in the Ardèche department north and east of Alès, for the birth. On the big day, my sister and I were parked with a babysitter who took us to a Catholic mass that lasted three hours. It was undoubtedly in Latin. At the ripe age of seven, I made a decision that the Catholic religion was definitely not for me and vowed never to set foot in a Catholic church again.

This lack of respect for Catholicism continued when we moved back to Brussels and, as a 10 year old, I heard that the Catholics went to the Congo to convert people to their religion. What bothered me most was the fact that the colonialists did not respect the culture of the Congolese. My search for increased understanding of different cultures and religions started at this time and later culminated in my professional work as a sociologist specializing in adjustment processes and African studies.

Argentina? Switzerland?

The only way to keep up with world news was to listen to the radio, as there were no newspapers, televisions or computers. After a while, the Germans started to interfere with the French broadcasting system; but they could not, at first, do so with the BBC from England. When they finally succeeded in blocking the BBC, my parents were able to listen to the Flemish stations, as all four of them were fluent in French, English, and Dutch, as well as German. When we were in Vialas this June, we heard from some of the people who had been in the Résistance that my parents were helping the Maquis to remain informed about world news.

By the end of 1942, the situation outside our haven was getting bleaker. Everyone was suffering. We were lucky to be in the unoccupied area of France, but Marshall Petain and his pro-Nazi Vichy government were now running the local police and the German demands grew ever more cumbersome for the families in our region. First, the Germans commanded the farmers to declare the size of their lands and to deliver all their cattle to the German army. Next, they rounded up all able-bodied men between 18 and 45 and sent them to Germany to work in the factories. They were replacements for the German men, who had been drafted as soldiers.

Problems also multiplied for Jewish families. My own life and the life of my whole family depended on the good will of every single person with whom we came into contact; for if any of us had been caught, we would have gone directly to a concentration camp. Now we children rarely went beyond our little village, as we were afraid that someone might ask who we were.

How about Argentina, my parents asked themselves? But there was no way to get there. I even heard them talking about sending all of us kids to Switzerland through an underground movement. In the end, they rejected this plan as unsafe, even though one of their first cousins was living there. They were wise again, as many of the transported children were caught by the Nazis and sent off to the concentration camps and ultimately gassed. Some local people with connections even tried to get visas for us to go to the United States, but that effort failed.

The Résistance

By this time, the Maquis or Résistance was building its strength, with camps of young people in abandoned houses burgeoning all over the area. My father and uncle participated in the movement and took part in a couple of acts of sabotage. For example, they once helped make 500 sheep on their way to Germany "disappear" overnight. My mother often repaired clothes for the young maquisars, and we children had to go occasionally to the camps to deliver messages.

Meanwhile, though, the noose was getting even tighter. By the beginning of 1943, while Churchill and FDR were already discussing the goal of unconditional surrender, the situation in France was deteriorating. The Germans seemed to be searching everywhere for those who were trying to escape deportation to Germany and, of course, for Jews.

Nine months after my brother was born, and at the end of the winter of 1943, the two fathers heard through Max that the local police had an order to arrest them. That same night they left the farm, at first staying in another village, in the house of the brother of the owner of the café in Soleyrols. The Maquis, which had organized a kind of housing bureau to find shelter for those who had taken refuge in the region, then hid the two brothers in a hamlet called Le Tronc, with Leon Guin and his wife. They lived in their barn until almost the end of the war. Le Tronc was not far from a main road, so the danger of discovery was great. Yet, without any thought of remuneration, this couple risked their lives in order to hide the two brothers and feed them three times a day. We children never saw our fathers. In fact, we were told that they had gone to Spain.

The Israeli government later decorated the Guins for sheltering my father and uncle along with other Jewish refugees. These and many other people who helped us were not seeking rewards but were acting from the bottom of their hearts with faith and courage. How grateful we were to the whole town and to all those in the area who took great risks to protect and care for us and who assumed, in so many different ways, responsibility for our welfare and survival.

Now my mother, my aunt and my grandmother, who

had been staying with us since my grandfather's death, had full responsibility for the farm and for us five children, ranging from a nine months old baby to my cousin and me, who were barely eight years old. The baby, in particular was creating a new challenge to the family, since we had no disposable diapers, toys, or pacifiers. My mother mashed his food and washed his diapers by hand. We siblings and cousins, tried to keep him entertained and often had to babysit him when the parents were working in the fields.

After the two fathers left, we had to take on additional responsibilities besides babysitting. Recently I uncovered an accounting book with my handwriting that started the day after my father left to go into hiding. I was supposed to count the number of eggs each hen laid every day and enter that data in the book my father used to keep. I am sure that we had other new duties, but I do not recall what they were.

We had a dog, Touté, and a cat, and two kittens, which had been born around the time my brother was born. The mother cat's duty was to keep the mouse population at bay, so when she was ready to go hunting, she placed her kittens between the paws of the dog and marched on her way. Another favorite place for the kittens was between Cristian's head and the back of the drawer in which he was sleeping. But it was the dog we loved the most, a black mutt, ever our faithful companion, who trotted beside us to school each morning and who was always there waiting for us at 4 o'clock when it was time to go home.

Second hideaway house

In Hiding

"They're coming to arrest you!"

Then a little while later, and I still remember that day, the daughter of the owner of the café in Soleyrols, Yvette Brignand, came running up the mountain—her face white as a sheet—to tell us that the police planned to come and arrest the rest of us. In her speech this June, Yvette reminisced about that event. A motorcyclist had ridden up to the café and asked her to carry an envelope to my mother and aunt in her bra and not to stop anywhere on the way to the farm. When she arrived at the farm, she found that her uncle was already there loading up our belongings in his cart and covering them with hay. Most of those belongings stayed in her parents' attic until we returned to Brussels. It took us less than three hours to say goodbye to the cats, kill the dog, grab whatever we could, and leave. My mother explained that we had to kill Touté because he would otherwise follow us, revealing our whereabouts to the Germans or their collaborators. We probably waited until dark so that no one would see us leave the farm.

The eight of us—our two mothers, we five kids, and my 65-year-old grandmother—no longer had the luxury of living together. At least, though, I could stay with my mother, sister Claudie, and baby brother Cristian. My mother, who was carrying Cristian, dropped him and he almost drowned that night. She had a bad boil on her arm which caused her to lose her grip on the baby when she slipped on a rock, crossing a stream. Max, our friend, grabbed Cristian and saved his life. Once more, death drew near us, took a peek, and then quickly moved on.

Our first home in hiding was with a wonderful family, the Guibals, who gave us their backroom and took care of us for over three months. When we arrived, Madame Guibal gave us a bowl of water with garlic and a piece of homemade bread. I remember my mother's look when I told her that I did not like that kind of food. She ordered me to eat it, as there might not be any more food for the rest of the day. And so, for three months, the four of us stayed in one room, keeping very quiet so the neighbors would not know we were there—never leaving that room except to the central courtyard and that was only possible late at night. We could not go anywhere outside the farm, even to school, for fear of being recognized and denounced by a collaborator.

All of the young men in the region were either in the war or in the Résistance, and the family's two daughters were still quite young; so the woman and her two daughters had to do all of the work on the farm. My mother helped those two girls, who were adolescents, go through a difficult period in their lives. I do not recall exactly what I did all day, but I do know that I read a lot. I had no way to pursue my schoolwork so, to keep my mind busy, I read the Bible from cover to cover several times. I have forgotten most passages, as I did not have much of a background to understand the book. I am sure my mother tried to teach me a little, but she was probably too busy with my brother, who was not even a year old, and my sister, who was only five. Of course, we had no toys or games. Even if we had found some kind of musical instrument, we could not have played it, since we had to be very quiet at all times. My husband and I still visit one of the daughters when we go to Vialas.

In the meantime, my cousin, Chantal, and my aunt hid in a schoolhouse on the second floor right above the only classroom. That meant no walking whatsoever while the school was in session so as not to raise suspicion. My aunt's younger son, who was four by that time, was placed with a family not too far from the school house. For more than a year, my aunt only saw him at night while he was asleep. He was said to be a cousin from Algeria because there was a collaborator living next door. That collaborator and his son were both killed one day, because the boy had been caught by a teacher making a map of Résistance camps in the region. Had they lived, it would have cost the lives of many members of the Résistance.

My grandmother first stayed with a family near my young cousin and then went to live with Madame Maurel in Alès, where she was known as Aunt Marie.

Le Saleçon

Living in one room with three little kids must have been miserable for my mother, so, after just three months, we moved again. A very warm and loving mother and daughter took the four of us into their home in a remote, two-family village named Le Saleçon, on the other side of the mountain. It was located a little closer to where the two fathers were. For my parents, aunt and uncle, who had been married for less than ten years that long separation must have been very difficult. There was no way for them to communicate except for occasional late night visits, when there was a full moon, as there were no telephones or other kinds of communication.

In Le Saleçon, both the mother and the daughter, Irenée Bastide, had been victims of the two world wars. Mamé, one of

the French words for Grandmother, had lost her husband
during the First World War and her daughter, Tata, the French
word for aunt, had a husband who was a prisoner of war in
Germany when we arrived. Down the mountain from us were
Tata's uncle and aunt. The husband, Tonton, the French word
for uncle, had been gassed during the First World War. The
only food he could digest was mashed potatoes and noodles. I
remember how hard it was for me to understand that, but it left
something in my mind that remained forever. The heartbreaks
and helplessness faced by these families was an incredible
contrast to the courage and faith with which they lived their
lives.

Since this village was a little more isolated, the three of
us children were allowed to go outside occasionally. After a
while, I was given a false name and a false identity card. My
new name was France Millard. At last, at the age of nine, I
could go to school again, but I had to learn to lie to survive. My
mother had always taught me to be truthful. How do you
explain such inconsistency to a child?

In some ways, life became routine. Every day, I would
put on my wooden shoes, the only shoes I had, and walk an
hour each way to the school on the other side of the mountain.
First, I went down to the river and crossed a makeshift bridge.
Then halfway up the opposite mountain, I would stop by a
particular rock and scream "hello" to Tata, who would relay
the news to my mother that I had crossed safely.

As France Millard, I was Tata's cousin, who had come
from a far-away town to get the mountain air. Since none of the
kids in my new school had ever known me before, my new
identity was credible. I don't remember making any friends
with my classmates, who were boys and girls from ages six up
to 18, again taught by one teacher in one classroom. One of the
older boys sang a song for me. The words are that the young
man is near a blonde girl and it is good to be near her and to
sleep with her. I was too young to understand the sexual
innuendos in the song, but strangely enough, I still remember

the words. It is true that I had a lot of blond curly hair. Going to a hairdresser was a totally foreign concept to us. Haircuts were done by members of the family.

A little later, my aunt and cousin came to live in our village. Fear was constantly with us, the gnawing fear that one day, just one collaborator would tell on us, or that a German or the local police would somehow see us and take us away. In fact, a lot of people knew about us but closed their eyes and did not talk about us.

We were told this June that local children were not informed about what was happening with our family for fear that they would be asked questions by collaborators. Yes, a few collaborators in other areas told the Germans about the locations of some of the Résistance camps, and a number of young men died in a couple of massacres. But there was a lot of trust in our small community—and an awareness of who the collaborators were. These collaborators were so despised that they were shot on the day the war ended.

Everyone around us was afraid too, both the villagers and the Germans. One day in the spring of 1944, Leon Guin from Le Tronc came running down the mountain to announce that some German trucks had stopped for the night on the main road at the top of the mountain, about an hour away by foot from the place we were hiding.

Everyone in our hamlet fled to the other side of the mountain, about a two-hour walk from the German overnight camp. All of us tried to sleep in a cemetery on the mountain that night, afraid that the Germans would come down and ask for food or harm us in some way. On the other hand, the Germans did not want any trouble either. Afraid of an attack by the Résistance, they kept their lights on all night and left the first thing the next morning.

Although I was too young to understand what was really happening to us, I could not escape the fear and the hatred all around me—we for the Germans and the Germans, I suppose, for us. I am sure that my parents, at the time, hated the Germans. Later, they were able to put aside that hatred and see that some Germans were caught in the same web that we were. My aunt, on the other hand, had a difficult time letting go of that hatred. She still cringed when my cousin, Chantal, and I made friends with a German girl after we came to the United States. She called Germans "Boche," a very derogatory name for the Nazis. In fact, my aunt barely accepted the fact that, in 1959, I received an invitation to go on a good will tour to Germany, Poland, and Austria with a group of young Quakers.

Quakers in France

My first acquaintance with Quakerism, which later became a great source of inspiration, came at this time. Tata was a Quaker and she used to take me to her Friends Meeting. People held the meetings in their own homes, and even then I was impressed by the silence and simplicity of their service—a great improvement over my earlier experience with the Catholic mass. I am sure that the Quaker way of thinking and life influenced Tata when she decided to take a family of four into an already poor household. Because we were hidden, we were not eligible to receive the monthly ration of staples as we did while we lived at La Font, so Mamé and Tata had to share their meager rations.

My uncle and my father on the
streets of Brussels before the war

Home Again

The Trip

By the late spring of 1944, we began to have hope, as
US and British troops landed in Italy. By the beginning of
June, they had entered Rome. Best of all, on June 6th, the Allies
launched the invasion of Normandy, and Paris was liberated
two months later. By that time, we were living a little more in
the open. We even had visitors—Max and his fiancée Fela, a
Polish fellow medical student. By early October, my father
made a trip to Belgium to assess the situation and returned with
news, both good and bad. The University would reopen in
November, some of our possession in Brussels had been stolen,
and…we had lost 64 members of our extended family in the
concentration camps. Some of them were the very same people
who had made fun of our parents for leaving their comfortable
life in Brussels just before the German invasion.

In November of that year, my father had to start teaching again at the University Libre de Bruxelles. With great sorrow, the five of us—my father, mother, sister, brother and I—left what had been our home for over four years. The trip was both painful and difficult. The trains were working in most places, but many times we had to go around bombed-out bridges in army trucks. On one of those trips, a man insisted on having me sit on his lap and took advantage of me. This was very traumatic for a 10-year-old girl. One night, we had to sleep on tables in the Paris railroad station waiting for the next train to Brussels.

Throughout the trip, there were no dining cars and no water in the toilets. Fortunately, our dear friends back in Le Saleçon had given us an enormous amount of food, which we stored above our seats. Once, in the middle of the night, I woke up feeling something sticky dripping down on my skin, my clothes, and my hair. It was honey from one of the containers that had not been closed tightly enough. Since there was little water, it took me quite a while to get cleaned; and it was a long time after that I was willing to touch honey again.

At the border between France and Belgium, my mother, who was carrying some of the left-over diamonds, was searched and threatened with a prison term. Why she was singled out and how she managed to escape, I just do not remember. By some miracle, we made it to Brussels and settled into a very small apartment.

Fortunately, by then, the Germans had already left Brussels, although they still were in the rest of the country. Food was scarce. My brother Cristian even caught pneumonia from the lack of heat in the apartment. I remember having to buy butter on the black market for him, from a farmer who was hiding it under flowers he was selling on the street. And then there were the bombs—the V-I and the V-II rockets which were constantly pelting the city after we arrived. Time and time again, the fire sirens announced that the V-1s were coming, and we scrambled for safety as the sirens wailed. Sirens bother me even today. But the worst bombs were the V-2s, which arrived without warning. One of them fell on a school in the neighborhood and killed a large number of children. Another fell on a movie theater and again devastated the neighborhood. Because of this, I can feel for the Iraqis who are going through a similar horror, not knowing if and when you are going to be hit next.

In December 1944, the Germans launched a counteroffensive in the Ardennes, called the Battle of the Bulge, and we all felt unsafe again, since Brussels was not far from there. And yet…and yet, everyone around us faced the Battle of the Bulge with hope, rather than despair. My parents were full of anxiety for themselves and their children, I am sure. But at the age of ten, I was not particularly concerned about the "situation." After all, instability and fear had been the fabric of my life for the past four years. I do not remember "Liberation Day," when everyone poured out into the streets to celebrate; but I can still picture the American troops in the streets distributing white bread and, best of all, one lemon for each of us children in Belgium. This was a great treat, as we had not seen a citrus fruit for more than four years.

Daily Life

When my uncle and Aunt came back from France, we were able to purchase a bigger house in the suburbs of Brussels that accommodated the ten of us. My grandmother had a room in the house next door but spent her days with us, helping with cooking and taking care of us.

School, though, was not much fun. Again, we were "different." For the last four years, we had lived in a peasant society quite different from the more sophisticated, urban culture of our schoolmates. Our manners were different, we had a southern accent, and the education we had received in the village schools was inadequate. I was put in 5th grade in a private school because of my age but I was far, far behind in most subjects. I am sure that my parents put us in a private school thinking that it would ease our transition but that was not necessarily the case. I did not like many of the courses but the one I hated the most was Flemish, which I did not think I needed, had never heard before, and the other kids had been learning since 1st grade. Unfortunately, it was a required course.

And so, for the first two years after our return "home," I was very unhappy. I don't remember making many friends, but at least I had my cousin Chantal, who is about the same age as I am. Despite the love and support we children received from our parents and from most of our teachers, our adjustment was slow and painful.

During the war, my aunt and uncle had decided that if they survived, they would adopt an orphan whose parents had died in the camps. Annie, our new adopted cousin, integrated into the family beautifully and she quickly became one of us.

In 1946, Chantal and I went to a public all-girls school for 7th, 8th and 9th grades. I started to make friends but I never was a very good student. After three years in an all-girls school, I still did not like the atmosphere, so my parents transferred me to another private school, this one for both boys and girls. I stayed there for one year before coming to the US. Our class of 15 had only three girls, which suited me just fine. Every day, to reach the school, I had to take a train for 20 minutes and then bicycle for a half hour. I had lots of girl-friends and boy-friends but we did not date, have birthday parties, or go to movies. I don't think I ever went to a movie until I came to the US, a year later.

My parents did not have much money but they succeeded in teaching us to ride bicycles and to swim. Also, we took modern dance classes where we learned to become a little more graceful, something that had not been emphasized when we lived in the mountains. In the summer, almost every year until we left Belgium, we went back to the Cévennes to visit our old friends.

When I heard classical music, almost literally for the first time after we settled in the bigger house, I begged my parents to buy me a piano, just so I could learn to play Bach. Weekly lessons and daily practice before school became a joyous part of my routine. Both my father and uncle enjoyed playing the piano so I did not feel too selfish.

A greater sorrow was just on the horizon—one that slowly crept into my consciousness and then totally changed my life. My mother had never talked to me about the lump in her breast. It was something she had had for a number of years and that neither she nor her homeopathic doctor had paid much attention to. True, she had had pneumonia in 1948, when I was 14. She would have died had it not been for the penicillin her uncle had brought back from America, a very recent US invention. The alarm I felt then subsided as she quickly recovered…or so it seemed.

In February 1950, my uncle and his family left for the US, crossing the Atlantic Ocean in five days on a ship called the Queen Mary. My uncle had a portable stamp business, so he could live anywhere. This was tough for me to lose my cousin with whom I was sharing so many things and even tougher for the family to arrive in a strange land where my aunt and uncle could easily communicate in English but my cousins could not.

That summer, my sister Claudie and I were sent to camp for a month while my mother recovered from what we were told was another bout of pneumonia. This was the first time that Chantal was not around so my sister Claudie and I became the best of friends, which had not taken place earlier and which we still are today. Because she was younger and tended to play with her younger siblings and cousins, I had not paid so much attention to her. After we came back from the camp, nothing was the same for us, as the severity of my mother's illness suddenly hit home. Worried about my mother, I began to gain weight. No one was giving me much direction about what to eat or not eat, although everyone teased me a lot about it. I was only 15 and I was so heavy that I could not run like the others for fear my bra strap would break. It took me almost 30 years to get my weight back to normal.

A picture from our first year in
Narberth, Pennsylvania, myself in the middle

The US

My parents started to think about emigrating to the US as soon as we returned home from France. Maybe they had never stopped thinking about it, especially since my mother's uncle, who had lived in the US, encouraged us to go there.

For some reason, they never discussed Canada, although some of my mother's uncles on her father's side had emigrated there. Maybe Canada was too cold for my parents. I wish I had asked about their decision when they were still alive.

Certainly, the future in Belgium seemed bleak—so

bleak that many young people were leaving for the Belgian
Congo as administrators or missionaries. The idea of
"remaking" the Congo in Belgium's own, more "civilized"
image became very popular, and photos of Congolese wild
animals and near-naked natives began appearing on the
wrappers of chocolate bars. Fascinated by this other world, I
too began collecting the wrappers and staring at the photos.

At the same time, I was very opinionated on the subject
of the European missionaries and had no use for anyone who
had the nerve to tell others what to do or what to believe. In
any case, my parents did not see Africa as a suitable future for
their children. So at the age of 50, my father and mother took a
big leap for our sakes and left Europe for the United States.
Ironically, both my brother Cristian and I later became
fascinated professionally by Africa and traveled or worked in
many of the French and English speaking countries on that
continent.

Cristian worked there most of his life in development
projects; and in the '70's, I traveled to 20 different African
countries giving lectures for the US government on American
higher education. In fact, I came back from one of these lecture
trips and recommended to the Department of State to institute a
system that would offer regular information on US education.
Now more than 220 cities around the world have Overseas
Advisers whose sole job is to advise international students
about the US and what it can offer to continue their education.

During the fall of 1950, my family arrived in the US on
the New Amsterdam, another of the main ships that crossed the
Atlantic Ocean, as commercial airplanes were still a rare
commodity. My father was one of the first professors to earn
recognition as a Fulbright scholar at the University of
Pennsylvania, where he taught chemistry for six months.
Philadelphia appealed to us, because Quakerism, which we still
admired, had a strong influence in this City of Brotherly Love.

Soon after we arrived, the two families, mine and my

uncle and aunt's, settled together in a small rented house in Narberth just outside Philadelphia. In a short time, we had our own roomy home, "Greenacres," in a nearby suburb of Philadelphia called Penn Valley.

Our parents were fluent in English, although the two fathers had very heavy accents, but for some reason they had never taught us children the language. Perhaps they wanted to talk about things they did not want us to hear. Or they were too distracted. I just don't know.

But I do know that adjusting to a new culture and a new language was rough. To top it all, the uncertainty about my mother's health gnawed at me once again. In 1951, after we had been in the US for only six months, my parents went back to Brussels for another six months—my father to teach as part of his Fulbright contract and my mother to get radium treatment. My sister, brother and I stayed with my uncle and aunt. I missed my parents a lot and, once again, had a hard time making friends. But at least we were lucky to be able to live with the other side of our family which we considered to be ours.

I was put in 11th grade, at Lower Merion High School in Ardmore, skipping 10th grade completely. Chantal, who is only 4 months older than I, took me to the high school and introduced me to most of the essentials of being a high school kid. Yet, I can only describe that year and a half in high school as miserable.

First of all, I knew only rudimentary English, so keeping up academically was very hard. Our social life was nonexistent, since 16-year-olds are usually not too open to newcomers. Even the everyday customs that my schoolmates took for granted seemed strange to us. The football pep rallies, which we were forced to attend, seemed barbaric to me, so I never went to a football game. None of the students invited us to their homes and we did not bring any of them to ours.

We did make friends with a German girl who was the only other foreign student in the whole high school. Chantal and I started going to the Quaker meeting in Merion, where we finally found young people with whom we felt compatible.

My Mother

Our family problems quickly became more serious than our social or school life. When my parents returned from Belgium, we could all see that my mother was not getting better. I remember very vividly my father's and uncle's faces when they came back from the specialist where they heard the news that her breast cancer had spread to her lungs. Three months later, in early 1952, barely a year after we had come to the US, my mother died.

How I missed her and still do. She was a wonderful model for all of us and had instilled in us all the right attitudes and morals. I always thought of her as a friend, rather than a mother. Because I had to be her helper from the time I was six years old, I have always been willing to take on responsibility. As a result, I became a leader later in life, just as my mother did. I enjoy doing things for other people, just like my mother. Both my sister, Claudie, and my brother, Cristian, also enjoy helping others—my sister through her Quaker meeting and her husband's position in Rotary International. My brother has spent his whole life helping people through his time in the Peace Corps and his career in international development.

History and Latin

Despite everything, I began to love a few courses in school. English as a Second Language did not exist at that time. Instead, the principal put Chantal and me in a top English class, so that the teacher could spend extra time with us. My favorite course was biology. Since most of our tests were multiple choice, I was able to study hard in advance and "ace the tests." The teacher probably did not realize that I spoke such poor English until one day I dared to raise my hand to answer a question. Latin was a bit easier. In fact, I could even converse with the teacher in Latin, since I had taken this subject in Belgium.

I absolutely loved American history, which I took in the summer between my junior and senior years of high school. History, as I knew it in Europe, was the story of kings and queens and their conquests—who reigned when and where and the battles they fought to get there. But American history! American history showed the development of ideas, particularly the idea that all people who want to pursue freedom and happiness are equal. I particularly liked the idea of the separation of church and state, which was not the case in Belgium.

During that summer, of course, college was on my mind. But who would accept me with an SAT score of 220—just about what you get from writing your name correctly? So, in addition to the American history class, I tackled English vocabulary, memorizing a book called "30 Days of Vocabulary." By October my SAT scores were much better, and I was accepted at both the University of Pennsylvania and Swarthmore College. Both were close to our homes. We knew that many American students go away to college, but we chose to stay very close to the family.

Swarthmore College

My cousin and I chose Swarthmore College mainly because of its Quaker influence and because it was between my father's job at Houdry Company and our home. This allowed him to stop every week on his way home so that we could chat.

Again, I had trouble academically; for example, I had to rewrite my first English 101 essay three times. Time and time again, I felt that my English was not sufficient to tackle university courses. But I didn't give up.

My social life was somewhat better than in high school, but not satisfactory. I took advantage of the wonderful opportunities that were available right on campus, like concerts, plays, and interesting talks. I dated a little but not as much as I would have liked. My friends were mostly very intellectual and were doing much better than I was, academically and socially. I always aspired to be in the Student Government but only became a leader in clubs like the Dance Club, the Young Quaker Group which I helped form, and the French Club. I did start a faculty and student club to take care of the growing number of foreign students who were studying at Swarthmore, as there were no foreign student advisers at that time. This was the beginning of my interest in working with foreign students.

I was active in the orchestra and the theater and also became involved in lots of other volunteer activities on campus and in the community. Even though there were more international students than in high school, I still felt like a foreigner. I was not that attractive, weighing over 150 pounds and feeling awkward about it.

Despite my academic difficulties, I graduated four years later. Both Brown University and the University of Illinois offered me assistantships in their biology master's degree programs, but I decided to take a job with the American Friends Service Committee in Philadelphia instead. For me, it was a wonderful job because I was working with an organization that was responsive to the needs of humankind at all levels. A year later, I moved on to Washington, DC, where I became assistant to the directors of Davis House, the Washington Quaker International Center.

As soon as I moved to Washington, I started to attend the Friends Meeting of Washington and became an active member of their youth group. About 15 of us young people did a lot of projects together. As a group, we invited four members of the Russian Komsomol, a youth organization, to travel around the US with us. Since we were the first group to invite a

Russian youth group to the US, coordinating with other organizations involved a lot of hard work. Some time in the early summer of 1958, we were even wined and dined by the US Senate Foreign Relations Committee. I will never forget that lunch, as I sat next to Senator Greene, who was in his 90's. I was the only woman in the group and during the luncheon, the illustrious senator from Maine slept half of the time and had his hand, groping my leg the other half. I was mortified and, being very innocent, I did not know what to do.

During the day, I worked as a glorified secretary to the directors of Davis House, but in the evenings and on weekends, I was able to participate in international seminars that took place at Davis House. Davis House is a Quaker International Center, managed by the American Friends Service Committee, which houses visitors from overseas. Many of those seminars were attended by such luminaries as Arnold Toynbee and William Fulbright. I was also active in International House, a residential facility for international and American students, located right across the street from Davis House. I felt very much in my element making friends with people from all around the world. Those two very exciting years made me decide to pursue a career in the area of international education.

France J. & Dean G. Pruitt – Circa 2000

Dean

The next summer, the Russian government reciprocated by inviting us to visit Moscow and to attend the 1959 Vienna Youth Festival. That was the Communist way of getting the youth together from all over the world. The Quakers were interested in being there, but only as observers. A decision was made by the Young Friends of North America to send four people to Russia and four to Poland before going on the Festival. I was lucky to be selected as the head of the team going to Poland. After traveling in England, Germany, and Poland, visiting other young Quakers, we arrived in Vienna at Quaker House. Since our group had arrived before most of the others, we took turns picking up people at the airport and the train station. One day, I had an intuition. "Something good is going to happen to me," I told my team. I didn't know what it was or exactly when it would happen, but somehow I was sure....

Not long afterwards, I heard that a young man named Dean Pruitt would be waiting at the airport to be picked-up. Even though it was not my turn, I told one of my team members that I wanted to go to the airport. Perhaps it was because I had heard about Dean or had seen him at some Quaker function before. Or because I vaguely remembered that his mother and my aunt knew each other. Our paths had almost crossed a few times, in different ways, but never long enough to have a conversation.

"I think I know your mother," were the first words I said to him at the airport. And that was the start of the most important relationship in my life. Until then, my career had been interesting, but my social life still left something to be desired. I had always said I would marry a Frenchman or a Quaker. But so far, no one meeting those criteria seemed just right. So when I met Dean, I could not believe that someone who had a similar philosophy and interests as mine could be interested in me.

If ever a couple seemed "made for each other," it was Dean and myself. The ten days after we met were a whirlwind. We went everywhere together—panel discussions, cultural activities, meals, excursions. We were both dedicated to promoting understanding among people regardless of race or religion. We were both interested in knowing more about the cultures of other countries, in trying to make peace with "the enemy."

All too soon, we were separated. Dean went on to a conference near Vienna and then to Northwestern University, where he was starting a post-doctoral fellowship. I went to Philadelphia, to start my new job as Program Assistant at the International House—a job for which I had been selected out of a group of 60 applicants.

"I think I met the man I'm going to marry," I told my

friend's mother when I stopped off in Amsterdam on my way home. Little did I know how soon that wish would come true. "I never want to be away from you for such a long time," I blurted out to Dean when we got together again. I had not planned to say such a thing, but it just came out. Now I knew which of the two alternatives—the Frenchman or the Quaker—I was choosing. Although we had been with each other for just about ten days, we both were sure. We decided right then to get married three months later, during the Christmas holidays. So by the time we got married, we had been together for less than three weeks and had known each other for less than four months. We never regretted our decision.

My Career

I moved to Evanston, Illinois, as Dean was a post-doctoral fellow at Northwestern University. I was able to find a one-year appointment with an international organization in Chicago and then persuaded Northwestern University to let me become their first foreign student adviser. There had been no one to work with their hundreds of foreign students and scholars on adjustment, language acquisition, immigration problems, etc.

In 1962, after Dean was appointed Assistant Professor at the University of Delaware, I persuaded the University to let me become their first foreign student adviser. This move east to Newark, Delaware, allowed us to be nearer to our families. We arrived there with our first child André, who was still an infant. Five years later, we had to find another location, as the University reasserted a nepotism rule that did not allow spouses to work on the campus.

Africa

Why Africa? I guess it started in my pre-teen years, in Brussels, when I had become so fascinated with the wild animals and native dancers on chocolate candy wrappers.

Later, as a foreign student adviser at the University of Delaware, I became friendly with a young Kenyan girl named Wambui, who soon became a good friend.

Wambui had come to the University of Delaware on a plane sent by President Kennedy, who wanted to encourage of African students to study in the US. She was one, the first African women to study in the US.

My fascination with my African students grew, especially since I could talk French with some of them. When we moved to the University at Buffalo, Dean became an associate professor. Dean accepted that position under one condition, that I would have a position as well. So a part-time position was created for me in the same year that the University appointed a full-time foreign student adviser. In the fall of 1966, the two of us opened the UB foreign student office. Again, like in most universities in the US, there was no one to take care of a growing population of overseas students.

By the time we moved to Buffalo, André was five and Paul and Charles, who were born in Delaware, were already four and two. We were lucky enough that a family with three girls moved next to us on our court. As each of these girls became a teenager, we hired her to take care of our boys when they came back from school. When our boys became teenagers themselves, they took turns cooking the evening meals. I had taught them how to cook from the time they were toddlers, as I was determined not to be alone in the kitchen. This training served them well when they became adults and had their own homes.

I began taking courses in anthropology and specializing in Africa. By the time I was accepted in an MA degree in anthropology, I was working full time. I also had three growing boys and a husband who needed my attention. I managed, though, by taking one course a semester. Dean helped me with exams and then with my master's thesis on the adaptation of African students to SUNY at Buffalo.

Because it was still unusual for women to work, I tried not to miss time for taking care of the children. Dean was the one who took the boys for emergency trips to the doctor or stayed with them at home when needed. Fortunately that was very rare as they were healthy kids. Between the three of them they only missed one week of school for their entire youth.

After interviewing over 60 African students at SUNY Buffalo, I concluded that students who learned about US customs and mores before they arrived adjusted better than those who learned about these subjects after their arrival.

In 1974, we went to France for nine months for Dean's first sabbatical. Before we left, I told myself that, by hook or by crook, I was going to go to Africa. First, I wrote a proposal for the Institute for Educational Planning of UNESCO to study the adaptation of African students to France. I was fortunate to be appointed a fellow for the year, one of the nine positions in that Institute for researchers from around the world. Unfortunately, the proposal did not get very far because I could not find a cooperative university or organization that would have enough participants for a significant research project.

While searching for more information on the adjustment of African students to France, I was put in contact with a diplomat in the US Embassy in Paris who had expressed interest in my master's thesis results. After discussing those results at a luncheon with him and his staff, the diplomat asked me if I would be interested in giving a series of lectures on US higher education and life on US campuses in a number of African countries where French and English were spoken.

That summer, we put the three boys in a camp in Spain, and Dean and I went to Tunisia, Kenya, and Ethiopia for two weeks. The Embassy was so pleased with my trip that I was asked to return to Africa four more times, giving French and English lectures in over 20 countries. At my recommendation and probably from others, there are now permanent staff members in each embassy. Whose main task is to inform and orient students who want to come to study in the US. Besides those trips, I worked on a contract with the Agency for International Development and the Department of Agriculture that took me to Morocco at least four times. And that is how my wish to visit Africa came true.

When we returned to Buffalo, Dean's work as a social psychologist became increasingly recognized. His research focused on the theoretical aspects of negotiation and conflict resolution, and he began writing textbooks which are now among the basic books used in undergraduate and graduate conflict courses around the world.

Buffalo, however, was not the best place for me. In 1976, the State of New York eliminated all international student adviser jobs. It was a tough time for me as I was not enjoying my new assignment in the Office of Financial Aid. Eventually, after two years, I found a job with the Agency for International Development (AID) in Washington, DC, and we bought a house in Bethesda, Maryland. I commuted for the first summer, and then Dean started to commute to Buffalo for 3 days a week, about 40 times a year. In the end, he commuted back and forth for 23 years. After a few years, all three boys were in college, which made it a little easier.

In some ways, a commuter marriage was a benefit for both Dean and me. Because we were separated for a good part of the week, I had a fairly independent life. I attended a number of professional events in the evening and went out to dinner with my friends. I was able to balance that life with one that fit with Dean's interests when he was at home.

I loved Washington when I came here first as a volunteer in a Quaker work camp a year after we arrived in this country, and then as a young worker at Davis House. I loved it when I came back for the AID job, and I still love it. After two years with AID, I opened the Office of International Programs and Services at George Mason University in Fairfax, Virginia, where I remained for seven years. So I am living exactly where I want to be.

The nicest thing is that Dean has always encouraged me to develop my professional life and then my business. In 1987, I opened a consulting firm in international education, called International Education Associates, and had many interesting jobs, including organizing a college for Japanese women and being appointed as its president for four months. Then the yen dropped and the project was discontinued.

For seven years, I worked for another Japanese organization called NCN, opening two offices in Washington and Philadelphia. Five years after I retired from NCN, I was asked to serve a six-year term as a director on the Board of their newly founded Foundation. I also work on a regular basis for the Agency for International Development and the Japanese Embassy. I continue to accept assignments here and overseas, though I no longer market myself.

Dean is also supportive of my volunteer activities in my professional organization, NAFSA: the Association for International Educators, where I chair the Embassy Dialogue Committee. In 1989, I became a member of the Bethesda/Chevy Chase Rotary Club a few months after the first woman was accepted into this international organization. I have been a very active member for the past 16 years and enjoy greatly working on Rotary's community and international projects. I am also active in the Friends Meeting of Washington where I ran their Bazaar for a number of years and participated in various committees.

Because Dean is not personally interested in these activities, I do not insist that he joins me in them. We enjoy being together, going to operas and movies, walks and bicycle trips, and on trips overseas, but we respect each other's separate areas of interest.

The family in 1993 – My uncle and aunt are in the center of the front row behind my son André, with his daughter Monica in his lap.

Forty-five Years Later

Family Life

By now, Dean and I have been married for over 46 years. And yet, what attracted me to him is still there. Dean has so many wonderful traits. I admire his intellectual knowledge and skills, easy-going attitude, warmth and understanding, and especially his way of always apologizing whenever he feels that he did not understand me or did something that I don't like. We just seem to be compatible in so many aspects of our lives. Best of all, Dean and I still share the desire to promote peace and understanding between people—the bond we found in each other from the very beginning.

Twenty-five years ago, I earned my doctoral degree in sociology from La Sorbonne in Paris, which has been of immense help in my career. Thanks to Dean's support, I was able to obtain the degree even though I was working full time and trying to bring up a family at the same time. He spent many hours helping me with my dissertation and taking on some tasks in the home to alleviate my work.

While our children were growing up, we enjoyed swimming, camping, going to Quaker meetings, and traveling as a family. I did not believe in being a taxi cab, so if the children were interested in taking lessons in music or art, I made arrangements for teachers to come to the house. I spent about half an hour with each child every night but did not have any special activities for each one.

Now we have three wonderful grown sons—André, Paul, and Charles—who are doing very well in their careers. The nicest thing for us is that they have decided to come back and live near or with us. Paul, the middle and single son, lives with us. The other two are married, so our family now includes two lovely daughters-in-law, Kim and Jane, who are great wives and caring mothers. Each family has two sweet and intelligent girls, our granddaughters. André and Kim's daughters, Monica and Erin, are now 13 and 10, respectively, while Charles and Jane's children, Katie and Jennifer, are seven and four, respectively.

I hope to leave a special legacy with Katie and Jennifer, as I have only spoken to them in French since they were born. The results are not perfect but they understand a good deal of what I say. On the other hand, they only receive things from me if they make an effort to ask for them in French. Much of the time, they speak to me in English and I answer in French and in English to make sure they understand what I am saying.

I went to help my daughters-in-law each time a baby was born, and I see all of our grandchildren on a regular basis, often to take care of them after school or if they are sick, so I feel close to each one of them. Dean and I try to do a variety of activities with our grandchildren—for example, going to the movies, the zoo, and the aquarium in Baltimore. However, going swimming with me seems to be the activity they all enjoy the most.

I guess the hardest thing about having grown, responsible children is to accept without question their ways of educating and raising their family. I know I have earned the respect of my two daughters-in-law because I rarely make suggestions—although I *do* ask a lot of questions. In fact, Kim once told me that she told her friends her mother-in-law was made in heaven! It may not be true, but I'm glad she feels that way. We try our best to relieve the young couples of their responsibilities from time to time so that both couples can have some extra time at work, for exercise, or recreation.

Greatest Challenges

Like all families, we have faced a number of challenges together, but in general we have been luckier than most families as we had three great kids who now live so close by. Most grandparents are not as lucky as we are.

The greatest challenge I face today is to keep in good physical and mental health so I can continue to do all of the things that I want to and not be dependent on someone else. In order to stay fit physically, I am at the YMCA daily either swimming or doing exercises. I also walk with Dean, and now Paul, for a half hour almost every evening. Being semi-retired, I have been able to work at a pace that fits my schedule. I still accept short-term jobs that require a lot of concentration, such as evaluating proposals for different governmental departments, and evaluating candidates for the Japanese JET program and the Rotary Ambassadorial scholarship program. In my spare time I read a lot about current affairs and an occasional book. I do try to keep in touch with many relatives and friends either in person, by phone, or by e-mail. I have been able to travel on my own in this country and overseas. I also go to Japan for the NCN Foundation from time to time and I enjoy that very much. Traveling with Dean is better but different, since I have more opportunities to meet people when I travel by myself.

My priorities are my husband, my children and their

families, my sister Claudie, my brother Cristian, my cousin Chantal, who is almost like a sister, and my many other relatives, friends and colleagues. I guess that my biggest surprise is that I am still alive at the age of 71 with only minor ailments. Both my grandmother and mother passed away when they were only 40.

Dean is retired but works three days a week at George Mason University, where he has been given the title of Distinguished Scholar in Residence. He is constantly being asked to write chapters and articles and to give talks. This new position requires occasional teaching but no more long distance commuting, which would no longer be comfortable in view of all of the present security requirements.

Quakers in the US

I have been connected with the Quaker movement all my adult life. Right after we arrived in the US, my family started going to Merion Friends Meeting with my uncle and aunt. A tree in honor of the four brothers and sisters was planted on the Meeting grounds by their six children.

I started the Student Meeting in the Friends Library at Swarthmore, and later was active in the Young Friends of Washington DC. After we married, Dean and I and three other couples started the Newark, Delaware Meeting, which is still thriving. We tried to establish a student meeting at SUNY at Buffalo, but unfortunately it is now defunct.

We are members of the Friends Meeting of Washington, which I attended as a young Friend. As a Quaker, I feel that I should put my beliefs into action. I am a concerned citizen and follow the local, national and international news pretty closely. I try to be as proactive as possible by contacting my senators and congressional representatives on issues that I feel strongly about.

Why the Quakers? Quakers do not all have the same beliefs. Some believe only in the absolute words of the Bible, others believe in Jesus Christ, and still others consider themselves Christians but have few explicit creeds. All of these beliefs are acceptable to me, but what I like the most in the brand of Quakerism that I belong to is that every person has a part of God in himself or herself and no minister is needed to worship God. As a result, we believe in working together for a common goal: peace. I share that hope for peace.

I still resent people who try to convert others to their own way of thinking. To me religion should be an individual choice.

Return to Vialas

Today, sixty years after the end of World War II, most members of the second generation continue to visit Vialas. Each time, we are amazed by how vividly the people of the region still remember how we came to them for help, and how they defied the invaders to save innocents impacted by the war.

In 2004, the six descendants of André, Denise, Alex, and Andrée donated a granite bench to Vialas as a gesture of thanks to the people of the Cévennes region, who literally saved our lives while endangering their own. The bench has been placed against the wall of the Huguenot Temple which is in the middle of the town. On the bench is inscribed, "In Honor of Those Who Welcomed the Refugees, Victims of the Oppression 1940-45, Gift from a Grateful Family."

On June 2nd, 2005, 16 members of our family—my sister and her family; part of my family, including Dean, two of our sons, one daughter-in-law, and two granddaughters; two of my mother's cousins from England and Switzerland; and the adopted son of my Uncle Francis—came to Vialas to dedicate the bench in a ceremony that took place at the Protestant Temple.

It was a very moving ceremony attended by over 100 people who came from all corners of France and from England, Switzerland and the US. Among them were about 30 children

from the local school. The Mayor wanted them to learn about
the accomplishments of their grandparents during the War.
Three separate people told me that June 2nd was the best day in
their lives. I gather that our family was the only one among the
refugees that had kept up their contacts with people of the
region. Offering something as concrete as a bench, where many
people will be able to sit and reflect about why it is there, was
very uplifting to them.

The master of ceremonies was Antoine Mercier,
Fanchon's son. After the Mayor's welcome words, speeches
were given by nine people: Fela Maurel, Max's widow;
Delphine Maurel, his granddaughter who read a speech Max
had written last year, just before his death; Fanchon Mercier;
Yvette Brignand Rota, who had run up the hill to tell us the
police were coming, so many years ago; myself; Claudie;
Christopher, Claudie's oldest son; Katie, our seven-year-old
granddaughter who read a poem she had written in honor of the
ceremony; and Jacques Freedman, my mother's first cousin. In
addition, three high school boys read poems about the War.
The ceremony ended with ringing of the Temple bells, after
which the municipality offered a cocktail party for all of the
attendees. Our family then offered a lunch at the Hotel Chante
Oiseau to the Maurel and Mercier families and other people we
knew well.

The speeches and our granddaughter Katie's poem are
presented at the end of the book, along with comments from
people at the luncheon, an article about the ceremony by
Fanchon , some pictures from the ceremony, some maps of the
region, and three family trees prepared by my son Paul.

For me, personally, there are not enough words to count
my blessings for having had parents with the wisdom and
foresight, the tenacity and courage, to seek out the wonderful
people of the Cévennes who showed such strength and
selflessness. I have gone through war, and I know how horrible
it is. But I also know, from first-hand experience that a little bit
of God is everywhere— even in some of the most isolated

places in the world.

Max and Fela Maurel (third and fourth from right) and friends in front of La Font, our first house of safety

Addendum A:
Talks Given at the Bench
Presentation Ceremony
Vialas, June 2, 2005

(In order of presentation)

Bernard Vignes, Mayor of Vialas

While wishing you welcome to our village, I would like first to thank the descendants of the J. family on two counts.

First to thank them for initiating this gesture of memory and gratefulness, which has come to fruition with the gift of this bench which we are inaugurating today. I imagine that it must have been difficult for you to relive the past.

Secondly I want to thank you for having bestowed this honor on the municipality and inhabitants of Vialas. The honor goes beyond the families who sheltered the Js, addressing all of those who, in this time of horror of the Nazis' oppression and the Vichy government, freely offered their solidarity and fraternity.

Thank you again for giving us the opportunity to remember with gratefulness the people from the Cévennes from La Font, Le Villaret, Le Salson, Le Penes, Le Tronc, and many other location for which history has not given us information about who existed and what they did.

We remember what they did and dared, fully conscious of the risks they and their families were running and the sacrifices they were imposing on themselves and their families. For example, the Guibal family of Le Villaret allowed a young man they had brought up to go for the obligatory service work for fear that his refusal would attract the attention of the authorities and thereby put in danger the refugees whom they were housing.

Yes, thank you for giving us, with the help of Max Maurel, unfortunately gone, and the Mercier family, this occasion to remember the men and women and what they did, without talking much about it even after the liberation, without boasting about it, simply being happy to learn later by the messages that were addressed to them, that those whom they had protected had found again a normal life, after a time when daily fear existed.

We are happy to meet you on the occasion of this visit like one is happy to find a distant relative.

This ceremony today is dedicated to the memory of, and with gratefulness to, those who were able to open their homes, their lives, and their hearts to the victims of the oppression. We will remember them, not to glorify ourselves but to emphasize the spirit and the values expressed in the refrain of the Cévennes which says endow your children so that they will follow them.

I hope that this day dedicated to memories will give us the privilege of remembering the best out of the worst of times.

Fela Maurel

I was hoping to read on my own, Max Maurel's remarks for this dedication. Max, my husband, had prepared them a few weeks before his death in October 2003. I wanted to read them for the memory that I have of this period and the fate that I shared during the war with this family whom I got to know thanks to Max. At that time he was my future husband and the Maurels were my future in-laws.

Unfortunately the brutal depart of Max has left me depressed mentally and physically; and with an accident I suffered a few weeks ago, I don't feel that I

can honor this reunion by reading Max's speech myself.
Hence, I have given that task to my oldest granddaughter,
Delphine Maurel. I am very sad that I cannot read it myself.

More than sixty years later, I am moved to find myself
among all of you who represent those who have survived
Nazism and who have kept unforgettable memories of the
Cévennes and this part of France. This region has known too
well the wars of religion, and it knows how to welcome people
and hide them from persecution.

Max Maurel (given posthumously by his granddaughter Delphine Maurel)

Vialas welcomes today André J's family, who came
from the United States with the wish to show their attachment
to the community where they lived during the four years of the
war. They are offering to the community a material good, a
bench in granite which will decorate, they hope, a public place.

In 1940, the J. family escaped from Belgium and
arrived in the south of France with the flow of refugees. How
and why did they arrive in Vialas?

Probably, they made a deliberate choice to come to the
Cévennes for geographic and historic reasons and also because
the pastor from Millau where they first arrived, advised them to
come to Vialas. There was little hope to go back to their
country of origin. This choice turned out to be a good one.

For the past 60 years, this region has always been the
destination of their children every time they come to Europe.
They want to see the region again and many of their friends
and acquaintances from the War.

The family settled in the farm called La Font which
they rented in Soleyrols. Coming from the city, the family was
not acquainted with rural and mountain realities. For the first
year, with the advice of their neighbors, they were able to grow

their crops and raise their animals. Their will of iron and their courage attracted the respect of their neighbors. André said to me one day after working hard, "Before this I had not known that my body had so many muscles and my pain is teaching me that."

In 1943, when the police made plans to arrest those hidden and those who were protecting them, the family spread around the area. André was settled near a camp of the Maquis, others were taken in charge by many families in the villages of the St. Frezal community.

Nevertheless, the memories of those years stayed with them. During those years, one of their members passed away, another one was born, their children went to school, they made friends, and the names of the farms, the villages, the paths, the roads were all familiar to them.

In the Cévennes, which saw so many refugees during those somber years, there are few examples of such a family, coming from far away in all senses of the word, who shared the work ethics and the values of the Cévennes.

I was well acquainted with André and Denise. This allows me to say that their relationships with those whom they knew, and let me mention some people like the Brignands, the Guibals, the Guins, the Benoits, the Velays, the Bonijols, and Pastor Burnand, were very close. André and Denise had a special spiritual character centered on their will, their energy, and their hope, overlooking the difficulties of their daily life. That spirit is animating their children.

Fanchon Maurel Mercier

History has already taught us that the Cévennes Mountains is a land of endurance. The events that we lived through during the greatest tragedy of the past century, already 60 years ago, have shown that the Cévennes Mountains are also a refuge for those persecuted: Jews running away from being rounded up, those who were against Nazism, and those in the Maquis or Résistance which organized many hiding places in the region.

In the year 1980, the Cévennol club started to collect information and testimonies on the Cévennol character, which descends from an unusual culture. In 1984 during a conference of historians, held in Valleraugue, we learned that in the Cévennes of the Lozère and the Gard, an area of about 20,000 to 40,000 inhabitants, with the majority being Christians, there were about 800 to 1000 Jews and other persecuted people. They were in the valley of the Cévennes, hidden and protected by the rural minority, with solidarity, without failure, and with the complicity of the local police. These people from the area, who spontaneously accepted to help, risked their lives for refugees they did not even know.

This research was not easy to accomplish because our people from the Cévennes don't like to talk about their actions, because of their modesty and maybe their sense of decency. Welcoming the persecuted seems normal to them. "We did our duty and nothing more" or "We could not have done it differently." It was as if they were making a modest contribution to a fight against the scandal that their conscience and their personal ethic prevented them from accepting. This aspect of the culture of the Cévennes was not overlooked by the J. family, and this is why for many long years before their definite departure to the US, the J. brothers and Andrée, Alex's spouse, came back loyally to see their friends from the Cévennes, making sure not to forget anyone.

André J., the professor, during one of his last visits, confided to my mother that these four years in the Cévennes, were on the human dimension, the most important years of his life and for that reason, unforgettable.

So thank you to the American descendants who are here today to express this duty of memory and gratefulness, which touches us deeply.

Yvette Brignand Rota

I was born on the 26th of September 1924 in Soleyrols, where my father was a road manager who also farmed our property. I was still living there in 1940 at the time of the arrival of the André and Alex's families, who came to live in the area, so they said, as farmers at the La Font farm.

Louis J., the grandfather, and his wife stayed across the road from where we lived in a little house that belonged to my parents. On the 6th of November 1940 Louis died suddenly. He is buried in the cemetery in Vialas. Later on, they put on his tombstone: "He lies in peace in this hospitable land."

At the farm, they did the best that they could with the daily chores of the garden, the animals, and the seasonal harvests, such as cutting grass by hand and collecting the chestnuts. We were often asked for advice. On a number of occasions my father Louis Brignand and my uncle Emile Brignand, known as "Tonton B" in the Résistance Movement, helped them to become farmers.

They hardly left the farm except to come down to see my parents or to get some milk. Instead they worked in the open fields and in the forests cutting wood.

My sister and I knew very little about what was going on, so there was a certain mystery about them. Our parents never spoke about the situation and we respected their silence. At times, we would go to La Font for an evening gathering, but as soon as we arrived, the young children were put to bed, so no information filtered down to us from them either.

We learned much later, after the Liberation, that a solid network existed around the family to watch out for their safety. Many people were ready to intervene, should they be in danger.

In February 1943, we were informed of a roundup of Jewish men. My father and my uncle took André and Alex to my grandmother's home at Le Massufret, where a separate room with two exits was waiting for them.

A month later, I was standing in front of my house, with a friend, when a motorcyclist stopped and asked to speak with me inside my house. He gave me an envelope which had been folded carefully, and asked me to take it up to La Font urgently. He said to me, "Hide it in your bra and hurry on up, and don't stop along the way until you get there."

I started to climb the mountain as fast as I could, only to discover that my uncle was already there, loading his cart with wooden boxes that contained a few of the family's belongings, which he later covered with hay. My family had been preparing for the exodus of the J. family.

On that same night, my father and my uncle with little Pierre on his shoulder would guide the group across the broom plants and the briars, descending as quickly as possible to the old mills, which stood at the bottom of the little bridge of Villaret, where my uncle was to pick them up at dawn and bring them further on. The days of worries and hope were over at Soleyrols.

But when I came back home that day, my mission was not over. Denise and Andrée had given me a text for telegrams to different people and different addresses, which said: "Send urgent white summer jacket for Yvette." The telegram receptionist in Florac thought that that it was strange to send the same message to different addresses without even signing it, but I insisted that she do so and it was accomplished.

The next day early in the morning, Brigadier Salager, having been informed of his duty, presented himself to us accompanied by two colleagues. He announced to my parents that he had orders to go up to La Font on a mission that was against his will. He regretted that he had to do it, but he did not tell my parents what it was. My parents listened to him without showing any emotion, and very calmly offered the trio some coffee. They knew that the officers would find the farm empty of its occupants except for a dead dog.

I must add that the late Leo Rousson, teacher and a member of our family, had attempted in August of 1942, with the help of one of our cousins who had a high position with the ministry of Finance in the Vichy government, to intervene with the American Embassy for a solution that would allow them to emigrate to that country. But that mission failed.

Dear friends, I am probably the only one alive today who can report to you these memorable experiences, and I am happy to be able to participate in this ceremony.

Since that time, members of your family have knocked many times at our house in Soleyrols and they have written to my parents as well. At the death of my mother, I took over from where she left off and never lost contact with Denise and Andrée. I realized at that moment, how much the Cévennol countryside meant to them, and how dear its inhabitants and my parents were to them.

It is with the greatest pleasure that we meet you today and that we can talk again about this difficult and tragic period, during which the hearts and arms united men and women from this welcoming country to win the battle for life and for liberty.

France J. Pruitt

Monsieur le Maire, André Platon, friends, children of the school of Vialas.

Words are really not sufficient to express my feelings of gratitude this morning, in front of this bench, which our family is donating, today, officially to Vialas as a symbol of our gratefulness toward the people of this area. Many of them were your grandparents, parents, and neighbors, who so courageously helped us and often sacrificed themselves to protect us. We owe them our lives.

I would like to tell you very briefly the story of a little girl who was born in the 1930's in Brussels and who lived in the Cévennes during the four years of the Second World War. This short story hopefully will help the younger ones among you to understand the role the people from the Cévennes played in my life and that of many other people. For those of you who are older, it will serve as a reminder of the many incredible things that took place over 60 years ago. This little girl is me.

For the first five years of my life, my life was very privileged and full of happy times. I lived in Brussels in a big apartment building across from a beautiful park. The streets had many stores, full of merchandise. My father was a university professor at the Free University of Brussels. My mother took care of me and my sister Claudie, who is sitting next to me. We had maids who also took care of us and we were always very nicely dressed. I liked to play in the park with my sister and my cousin Chantal. In the winter, we went to Switzerland to ski, and in the summertime, we went to the Belgian coast.

Suddenly, in May of 1940, my life and that of many others changed, as the Nazis had invaded the Scandinavian countries, the Low Countries, and part of France. My family was a bit different from others as two brothers had married two sisters and we always lived together. For a number of years, the two young couples, who had been observing the development of Hitler's power and the mentality of the Nazis, decided to leave Belgium if it was invaded. Twenty-four hours after the invasion of Belgium, the family drove out of Belgium in a large car with a trailer behind that contained all of our worldly possessions. In the car were my paternal grandparents, my father and his brother, my mother and her sister, and we four children who were all under six. We were one of the last cars allowed to enter France as the border closed when too many refugees tried to escape to France. This departure was the beginning of an adventure that turned out well but could have been disastrous if we had not decided to stay in Soleyrols, a

small hamlet near Vialas in the Lozère Department, which was
in a non-occupied area of France.

After a short stop in Bèdoues, the two families settled
in an isolated abandoned farm, La Font, located 20 minutes up
the mountain from Soleyrols. The farmers of the area taught us
how to cultivate the land, to plant and collect the vegetables, to
raise the goats, rabbits, pigs and bees, and to pick up the
chestnuts. And I still like the Bajana (dried chestnut stew
which takes over two hours to cook but is very sweet and
tasty).

I remember well going down to Soleyrols every day to
school, accompanied by my cousin and our dog Touté who
returned in the afternoon to pick us up. M. André, our teacher,
was alone in trying to instruct 15 to 20 of us whose ages ranged
from 6 to 18.

For the first two years of the war, the Nazis continued
to conquer more of Europe. They ordered all capable men in
these areas to go to Germany to work in the factories. At the
same time, millions of Jews, handicapped people, and
homosexuals were sent to concentration camps where most of
them were exterminated. The Germans wanted a pure race.

But we felt secure in our farm thanks to the many
people who had become our friends. Among those friends were
Mme. Suzanne Maurel and her two children, Fanchon and
Max, aged 16 and 18, who often came to visit us at the farm.
We are so pleased that Fanchon and Max's widow, Fela, are
here with their children and grandchildren to celebrate this
event with us.

Then suddenly, in February 1943, my father and my
uncle had to hide as the Résistance had heard that the police
were going to come to pick them up. In order not to worry us
children, we were told that our fathers had gone to Spain. In
fact, they were hidden in the barn of the Guin family, which
was about three hours walk from our farm. That family was

honored by the Israeli government for having sheltered a
number of refugees.

A little while later, the pastor from a nearby town let
the Résistance know that the police was ordered to pick up the
rest of the family. I still remember the face of Yvette Brignand,
who came running up the mountain to announce to us that we
were next on the list. With the help of Yvette's family and Max
Maurel, we evacuated the farm in a couple of hours, and that
night we left for our new homes. Our worldly possessions were
taken away in a horse cart under a load of hay and stored in the
Brignand's attic. The saddest event for us was that we had to
kill our dog, so that he would not follow us. The next day,
policemen came to the Brignand's café and told that family that
they were there to do the saddest thing they ever had been
asked to do. They drank a lot of coffee, hoping that someone
would run up to the farm to warn us. They were much relieved
to find an empty farm with a dead dog. That night, my brother
who was nine months old, almost perished when my mother
slipped on a rock and almost dropped him into a stream.

Thanks to the Maquis, eight members of our family
were received in four different homes in the area surrounding
Soleyrols. Our first refuge was that of Mme Guibal of Villaret
and her two daughters, Alice and Simone, who received us so
warmly. They hid us in their back room and fed us for over
three months. We did not have any toys, no television, no video
games, and we could not play outside except late at night for
fear of revealing our presence to the neighbors and the workers
in the mines across the mountain. I loved to read but there were
no libraries, so I read the Bible several times.

Soon the Maquis decided to move us, as the location
was not appropriate for three children. We were placed in Le
Saleçon with Irènée Bastide and her mother who also received
us with opened arms. We remained there until the end of the
war, 18 months later. This little village was more isolated, and
the other inhabitants, the Chabrols, understood our problems.
After four months, I was able to go to school in Vimbouches,

an hour's walk, on the other side of the mountain from where we lived. I went under a false name. I was called France Millard and I had a false identification card. And my parents had always taught me not to lie! Gradually the other members of the family came to Le Saleçon except for my grandmother, who stayed with Suzanne Maurel in Alès. She became Aunt Marie but she did not leave the house for almost two years.

Another memory that I have which was very scary is that one early evening, a convoy of Nazis trucks stopped on the route of the Crêtes, which is located at about an hour's walk from Le Saleçon, to repair one of their trucks. There was panic in the village, as everyone thought that they would come down to ask for food or to kill us. We all slept in the cemetery in Vimbouches and nothing happened. The Nazis were probably also afraid as they knew that the Maquis was getting stronger in the region. In the area of Vialas, the Nazis or the collaborators were unable to locate the camps, but some camps in other regions were destroyed and many young people in them were killed because they were denounced by collaborators.

Finally in June 1944, the allies arrived in Normandy and the end of the war was on the horizon. Our father visited Brussels and found that 64 members of our family had perished in the concentration camps. Meanwhile my family was alive thanks to the people of the Cévennes who had protected us and had risked their lives to save ours. They could have been caught hiding refugees and been deported or killed on the spot.

In November 1944, my father had to go back to teach at the University in Brussels, and we of course went back with him. This was very sad for us children because we were feeling very comfortable in the Cévennes. It was our home.

Our departure for Belgium was again very emotional. Our friends had given us enough food to survive for a week. On the train, unfortunately, péchère (the patois word for poor you) I woke up covered with honey as one of the jars had not been closed properly. There was no water on the train so I stayed sticky for many hours. For a long time, I was not able to eat honey.

And this is how a slice of this little girl's life, about whom I spoke to you at the beginning of this talk, ends. This little girl was extraordinarily, lucky in that her parents made the decision to leave Belgium and to live in the area around Vialas.

This bench, made out of the granite of Vialas, is a humble testimony of our recognition to you and our gratitude for all that you have done. On behalf of our parents, M. André and Mme. Denise, who are no longer alive, their brother and sister, who are also gone, their six children, and two of them are here, their eleven grandchildren, and four of them are here, and their ten great grandchildren, and two of them are here, thanks again to all of you, a million times, not only for what you did for our family but also for humanity. Wars exist but there are also incredible human beings who want peace and tranquility and care about other human beings. Your courage, and that of many who are no longer here, your completely altruistic behavior, saved the lives of ten people. We will never forget Vialas, the Cévennes, and France, and we will be eternally grateful to all of you.

Claudie J. Brock

Good morning, Mr. Vignes, good morning ladies and gentlemen and friends from the Cévennes. My husband Lynmar Brock, our son Christopher, and our son Andrew and his fiancé Alexandre Huebener, are here to visit you and to present to you our gratefulness. I will never forget your kindness, your generosity, your openness, and your courage.

For example, when our grandfather died at the beginning of the war, the people of the village of Soleyrols gathered to give moral support to our family, as we did not have much family here. They walked in the funeral procession

all the way from Soleyrols to Vialas, where our grandfather
was buried in the Protestant cemetery. And on his tomb is
written, "Here lies Louis J. in this hospitable land." He
remains here forever in your lovely community.

I will never forget when we had to run away from La
Font. Max Maurel came in the middle of the night to get us, in
order to take us where we were going to hide. It was winter, it
was dark, it was cold and we could not make any noise in order
not to alert the neighbors. There was ice on the grass and my
mother who was carrying my little brother in her arm, slid on
the ice and our little brother Cristian almost fell. If it was not
for Max, he would have drowned.

After the war our parents took us to Philadelphia in
Pennsylvania, in the US, where the great Quaker William Penn,
in the 17th Century, had opened the doors of his colony to those
who were persecuted for their religious beliefs. There they
could live in liberty and in peace. A bell which is found in
Philadelphia has become the symbol of US liberty. On this bell
is inscribed a passage from the book of Leviticus, "So that it
would announce liberty around the world." Today we are
bringing you a copy of this Liberty Bell, because you also
fought for your liberty. Mr. the Mayor, would you accept for
Vialas this present from the family of Mr. André and Ms.
Denise as a sign of gratefulness for all that people from here
did for us.

In my heart, there is a link that has been woven between
you and us, and in my memory is a deeply engraved
gratefulness, because, thanks to you, we are here today.

Christopher Brock

I am in front of you, not only because of the spirit of the
Cévennes, but also because you and your ancestors helped my
parents from my mother's side to survive the Second World
War.

The experiences of the J. family at La Font, where they

became farmers and where they discovered a way of living and surviving, has changed a lot of the identity of the family. In the Cévennes, they found sincerity, warmth and the simplicity of living, which they followed the rest of their lives.

After the end of the war and after my family emigrated to the United States, they chose a region near Philadelphia, where there were many members of the Society of Friends (Quakers). I think that my family chose to become Quakers because it is a religion similar to the religion of the Huguenots. Furthermore, if the two J. girls had not become Quakers, I doubt that France would have found Dean, a Philadelphia Quaker, and Claudie would not have found Lynmar, another Philadelphia Quaker. And without doubt, my cousins, my brother and I would not have arrived in this world. To the Cévennes spirit, we owe you so much and thank you profoundly.

Katie Pruitt

(see Addendum B)

Jacques Freedman

Dear friends, I am a cousin of France and Claudie who used to live in Belgium before the invasion by the Nazis. My parents, my sisters and I were also refugees in the south of France from May 1940 until March 1942. We were in Limoux in the Department of the Aude. We did not feel secure there because the local population was mostly pro-Vichy. Thanks to the courage of our mother and money from an aunt, we bought visas to leave France finding refuge in England. When we heard that the J. family was hidden in the Cévennes, we were relieved.

I had an opportunity to see my cousins before they emigrated to the US, and since that time, I have been impressed by the courage of the people of the Cévennes. This courage for the protection of minorities is due in part to your ancestors, the Vaudois (disciples of Pierre Valdo), who were persecuted by

François the 1st, and your other ancestors who chose the route of reform, but at such a price and such sacrifice until the time of the French Revolution.

A lot has been written about the "Righteous Ones" in France especially those from the Cévennes. Had they all been recognized by Israel, one would find a forest of chestnut trees planted by the "Righteous Ones" in Yad Vashem. This is the reason I wanted to attend this celebration to meet the "Righteous Ones" and to say thank you in all sincerity.

Addendum B:
Poem Written and Read
by Katie Pruitt at the
Bench Presentation Ceremony

My Dreams

What dreams do you dream?
Do you dream about making whip cream?
Some people dream about trains with steam.

I dream of evil about to scream!!!
And about my soccer team.

Some people dream about jello...
Others dream about the color yellow.

Some people dream about bats.
Others dream about hats.

Some dream about acrobats.
Some dream about cats.

Some dream about houses.
Others dream about mouses.

Some dream about tea.
Others dream about not being able to see.

Some even dream about scrapes on their knees.
And if you please, you can dream about peas.

Some dream about trees.
Others dream about the breeze.

Some dream about a beautiful dress.
If you were the best, you would dream about stress.

Some dream about tables.
Others dream about labels.

Some dream about walls.
Others dream about halls.

Some dream about lights.
Others dream about fights

Some dream about beds.
Others dream about heads

Some dream about a curtain.
Others dream about being certain.

Oh please, please tell me what you dream.
It's not like what it seems.

Addendum C:
Remarks Made by
Guests at the Luncheon

Jean Lamorthe

I was 6 years old in 1940 and I remember Pastor Burnand who used to come at night, to fetch my uncle, Marc, for missions on the other side of the mountain (St. André, St. Frezal), which children of our age did not understand

Jean Rousson

Joy to remember my younger years. Incredible day full of memories and friendship.

André Platon and Louise Platon

Marvelous day full of memories and friendship. Thanks for having allowed it to take place.

Etienne Passebois, Mayor of St. Frezal

Andrée J's pink dress is a strong memory of my childhood.

André Hours

What an immense happiness you have offered us. I am able to relive with your little girls, the little Pierre in those somber years so rich in memories. I have transmitted those memories to my children so that they don't forget, through all of those memories, that some poor innocent people were persecuted to death. To all of you and your families whom we will never forget, a huge thank you, doubled by my infinite friendship.

Bernard Vignes, Mayor of Vialas

Much better than a ceremony. It is a meeting with those whom we only had heard about and whose friendship warms our hearts even if it is from far away.

François Maurel, son of
Max and Fela Maurel

Time and the oceans don't minimize the memory, the love and the hope for the future generations.

Jacques Freedman

Thank you for this meeting of the two continents. To become acquainted with the people from the Cévennes was moving.

Benjamin Richmond-Freedman,
cousin of France and Claudie

What a fantastic meeting and memories. As far as I am concerned, it was discovering my family. I discovered Vialas, and by these moving speeches, I understood the fate of the J.s which has become an integral part of this village.

Anissa Ghariani, granddaughter of Fanchon

I was very happy to have had the occasion to be present at this ceremony. I hope to see you soon in the US. I will keep you informed.

Nadia Ghariani, granddaughter of Fanchon

I don't regret at all to have made that long trip. The ceremony was very successful and moved me a lot. I was happy to have seen you again. Your family is adorable and I love you all a lot. It was a superb weekend. Thanks for all.

Isabelle Mercier, daughter of Fanchon

Superb day, unforgettable. Moving and so well organized, my dear Tata France.

Justine Maurel, granddaughter of Max and Fela

So happy to have met you. I hope to see you soon.

Fanchon Mercier

My dearest American sister. June 2nd was very good and beautiful. Thank you to all and see you soon.

Cosima Maurel, Max and Fela's daughter-in-law

Delighted to have seen you on this magnificent summer day, unforgettable for us and for the future generations. May they continue even when we are no longer here.

Katie Pruitt

I am so happy to be here. It is kind of nice to meet family and new friends. I know all the kids paid attention to my speech. I am so happy to have you as my grandmother.

Jane Pruitt, Katie's mother

Thanks so much for organizing this event in Vialas.

Charles Pruitt, France's son and Katie's father

Before now, Vialas and its people were distant, mythical concepts that were subjects of family stories of our past. Now, after my first visit and the ceremony, Vialas, the Cévennes region and its people have become real and I have experienced all its kindness, beauty, and greatness. This has been very moving and I am grateful for the experience.

Fela Maurel

What a joy to see all of you here with us. So many years have passed since our first meeting. Many dear ones have disappeared. But this big family whom I knew during the war changed my life. Life continues with all its joys, happiness, and sorrows as well. I had the chance to know you thanks to Max, who became my beloved husband. His family replaced in part mine, who disappeared in Poland. I will think about that until the end of my life. I kiss you very hard, very affectionately.

Addendum D:
Article by Fanchon Mercier
in <u>Les Nouvelles Cévennoles</u>

An homage to the people from Lozère, who during the black years of 1940-44 helped and protected those who were threaten with persecution by the laws of the Nazi government in the countries that had been occupied by the German army, was celebrated on June 2nd in Vialas, at the initiative of a family of Jewish origin who were hidden in the region.

The celebration was organized by the descendants of the J. family, who escaped Belgium in 1940 and after a long and complicated journey, landed in the community of Vialas, where they stayed until the liberation, thanks to the solidarity without failure of the rural families, who, even endangered their lives, harboring and protecting this family of 10 people for more than 4 years.

The J. descendants moved to the United States but never forgot that they owed their lives to the inhabitants of the Cévennes, and manifested their gratitude by offering the community a granite bench which 16 people of their family came to inaugurate on June 2nd.

They were welcome by the mayor of Vialas, with the Mayor of St. Frezal de Ventalon (the community that also harbored some of the family members from 1943 to 1944) and the descendants of the people from the village of Soleyrols where they lived between 1940 and 1943.

Many people of Vialas attended this very moving ceremony of memories during which a few speeches were given, and in particular by Mrs. France J. Pruitt who evoked the memories of those 4 years of her Cévennol youth (she was between the ages of 5 ½ and 10). She concluded by saying, "Your altruism saved the lives of 10 people who will never forget Vialas, the Cévennes, the department of Lozère and the country of France."

Addendum E:
Pictures from the Bench
Presentation Ceremony

View of Vialas

Bench Donated to Vialas

Protestant Temple in Vialas

Mayor Bernard Vignes

Antoine and Fanchon Mercier

Fela and Delphine Maurel

Yvette Brignand Rota

The Author

Claudie Brock

Christopher Brock

Jacques Freedman   Katie Pruitt Reading Poem

Part of the Audience at the Ceremony

School Children Were Also in the Audience

Katie and Jenny Uncovering the Inscription
with Help from the Mayor and the Author

High School Students Reading Poem about the War

Our Family on the Bench after the Ceremony

The Mountain behind Vialas

La Font Today

The Inscription on the bench. The flash makes
part of it hard to read. Below is a Photoshop-aided
rendition of the text with the English translation.

EN HOMMAGE
A CEUX QUI ONT
ACCUEILLI LES REFUGIES
VICTIMES DE L' OPPRESSION
1940 - 1945
DON D'UNE FAMILLE
RECONNAISSANTE

"IN HONOR
OF THOSE WHO
WELCOMED THE REFUGEE
VICTIMS OF THE OPPRESSION
1940 – 1945
GIFT FROM A
GRATEFUL FAMILY"

Addendum F:
Maps

Map of France

As you can see, Vialas is in
the middle of southern France.

Map of Lozère

Vialas is in the southeast of Lozère,
one of the 95 departments of France.

Map of Vialas and Soleyrols

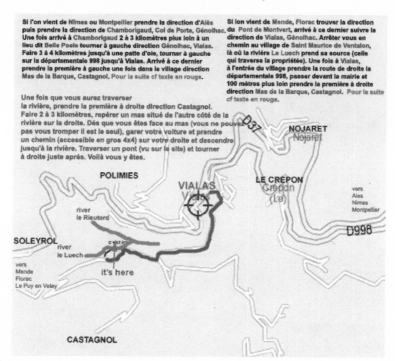

Si l'on vient de Nîmes ou Montpellier prendre la direction d'Alès puis prendre la direction de Chamborigaud, Col de Porte, Génolhac. Une fois arrivé à Chamborigaud 2 à 3 kilomètres plus loin à un lieu dit Belle Poele tourner à gauche direction Génolhac, Vialas. Faire 3 à 4 kilomètres jusqu'à une patte d'oie, tourner à gauche sur la départementale 998 jusqu'à Vialas. Arrivé à ce dernier prendre la première à gauche une fois dans le village direction Mas de la Barque, Castagnol. Pour la suite cf texte en rouge.

Si lon vient de Mende, Florac trouver la direction du Pont de Montvert, arrivé à ce dernier suivre la direction de Vialas, Génolhac. Arrêter vous en chemin au village de Saint Maurice de Ventalon, là où la rivière Le Luech prend sa source (celle qui traverse la propriétée). Une fois à Vialas, à l'entrée du village prendre la route de droite la départementale 998, passer devant la mairie et 100 mètres plus loin prendre la première à droite direction Mas de la Barque, Castagnol. Pour la suite cf texte en rouge.

Une fois que vous aurez traverser la rivière, prendre la première à droite direction Castagnol. Faire 2 à 3 kilomètres, repérer un mas situé de l'autre côté de la rivière sur la droite. Dés que vous êtes face au mas (vous ne pouvez pas vous tromper il est le seul), garer votre voiture et prendre un chemin (accessible en gros 4x4) sur votre droite et descendre jusqu'à la rivière. Traverser un pont (vu sur le site) et tourner à droite juste aprés. Voilà vous y êtes.

Here you can see Vialas and Soleyrols and
how winding the mountain roads are.

Map of Nearby Major
Cities and Regions

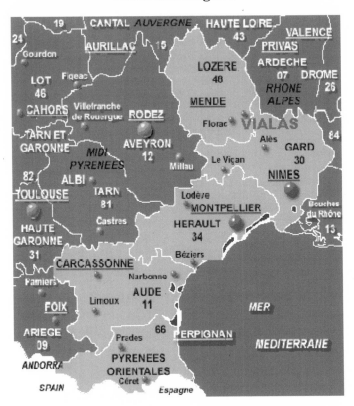

This map shows how close Vialas is to the
Mediterranean and to Nimes, Montpelier, and Spain.

Addendum G:
The Author's Family Tree

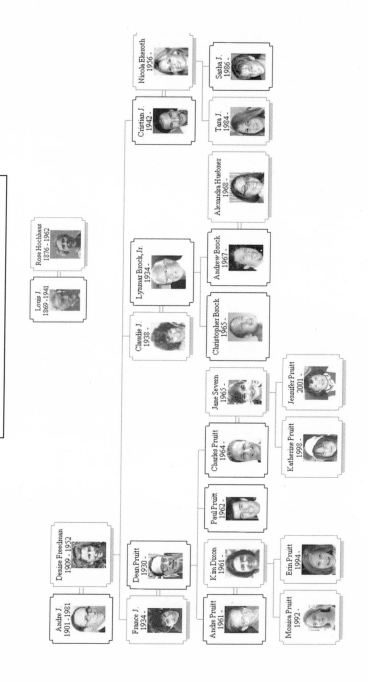

Descendents of André and Denise J.

Rose Hochhaus
1876 - 1962

Louis J.
1869 - 1941

Nicola Ekeroth
1956 -

Cristian J.
1942 -

Sacha J.
1986 -

Tara J.
1984 -

Alexandra Huebner
1968 -

Lynmar Brock, Jr.
1934 -

Claudie J.
1938 -

Andrew Brock
1967 -

Christopher Brock
1965 -

Jane Severn
1965 -

Charles Pruitt
1964 -

Jennifer Pruitt
2001 -

Katherine Pruitt
1998 -

Paul Pruitt
1962 -

Denise Freedman
1909 - 1952

André J.
1901 - 1981

Dean Pruitt
1930 -

France J.
1934 -

Kim Dixon
1961 -

André Pruitt
1961 -

Erin Pruitt
1994 -

Monica Pruitt
1992 -

Printed and distributed by:
Lulu.com
To order more copies, please go to:
http://www.lulu.com/content/155537